PLAXTON: THE PANORAMA AND PANORAMA ELITE YEARS

HOWARD BERRY

AMBERLEY

First published 2024

Amberley Publishing
The Hill, Stroud
Gloucestershire, GL5 4EP

www.amberley-books.com

Copyright © Howard Berry, 2024

The right of Howard Berry to be identified as
the Author of this work has been asserted in
accordance with the Copyrights, Designs and
Patents Act 1988.

ISBN 978 1 4456 7929 7 (print)
ISBN 978 1 4456 7930 3 (ebook)

British Library Cataloguing in Publication Data.
A catalogue record for this book is available from
the British Library.

Origination by Amberley Publishing.
Printed in the UK.

Contents

Introduction

Originally founded in 1907 by Frederick William Plaxton, the company which today is Britain's only mainstream coach bodybuilder began life as a joinery workshop in Bar Street, Scarborough, the Yorkshire town in which it is still based today. The company soon expanded into construction and built several notable buildings in its home town. Shortly after the end of the First World War, the company diversified into building charabanc bodies on Ford Model T chassis and car bodies, primarily for Crossley (F. W. Plaxton having established a strong business connection with William Malmesbury-Letts, Crossley's Managing Director) but also on chassis such as Daimler, Rolls-Royce, and Sunbeam. The depression of 1929 to 1933 made the manufacture of luxury automobiles difficult and so the construction of charabanc bodies became vital to the company. Incidentally, the first motor bodybuilding premises was called Castle Works as it looked out onto Scarborough's Castle Road, and for many years since, the castle symbol was Plaxton's emblem.

By 1936, the company was successful enough to justify the construction of a large new manufacturing facility in Seamer Road, Scarborough, and this allowed for an increase in production which helped Plaxton bodies become popular with numerous independent operators across the UK. Rather than ordering directly from the factory, many operators purchased their vehicles through independent dealers, and most of Plaxton's sales were through Lancashire Motor Traders Ltd of Manchester and Arlington Motor Co. Ltd of London. In 1937, the company became known as F. W. Plaxton & Son as Frederick Plaxton's son (also named Frederick William) joined the company at the age of eighteen, Mr Plaxton junior being known as Eric to avoid confusion with his father.

At the outbreak of the Second World War in 1939, bodywork production was suspended and Seamer Road was turned into a munitions factory under the control of the Ministry of Aircraft Production. In 1943 an incendiary bomb struck the factory, and the resulting fire resulted in the loss of many of the company's early records. As the factory was under control of the Ministry of Works, munitions production continued in the open air whilst a replacement factory was constructed and land adjacent to Seamer Road was loaned to the company by Mr C. F. B. Quarton, a market gardener who subsequently joined the Plaxton board. Bodywork production restarted at the end of 1945, and in 1951 the business was registered for the first time as a private company, Plaxton (Scarborough) Limited.

In 1957 the founder of the company, F. W. Plaxton Senior, died, and was succeeded as Chairman by his son Frederick Junior. In 1961, Plaxton became a public company, an event which coincided with the opening of a brand-new factory on a 45-acre site at Eastfield on the outskirts of Scarborough. Joint Managing Director Mr Tom Stephenson, realising what a major player in the bodybuilding market the company had become, saw that expansion was the way forward. The logical layout of the new factory made the building process more efficient and with Seamer Road able to concentrate on vehicle finishing, Plaxton products became highly competitive in both price and specification. This popularity led to the downfall of a number of smaller bodybuilding concerns, and in 1963 the premises of W. L. Thurgood of Ware in Hertfordshire were acquired, and for many years acted as a service and repair depot for southern England.

Plaxton travelled through the 1960s and '70s as the leading bus and coach bodybuilder in Great Britain, with new vehicle registrations constantly over 1,000 vehicles per year. As an example, 1973 saw 1,300 bodies built, one third of the entire UK single-deck bus and coach production figure. The company achieved this strong position not only due to the quality of its products, but by introducing modern new designs able to be built on time and to the customer's specification at the efficient Eastfield plant.

The 1980s were a decade of major change for Plaxton, starting in 1980 with the acquisition of T. H. Burgess (Holdings) Ltd, which brought the Pilsley-based (Chesterfield) concern of Reeve Burgess into the fold. Reeve Burgess had made its name in the late 1970s with the rather angular Reebur range of mini-coaches, which included seventeen-seaters based on Bedford CF and Ford Transit chassis up to a twenty-six-seater on the MAN 8.136 chassis. Thus, the Plaxton and Reeve Burgess ranges complemented each other, and production of minibuses and coaches at Pilsley continued until the factory was closed in 1991 – a downturn in the full-size coach side of the business meant space for the Reebur range to be built at Scarborough. At the end of 1986, the Kirkby Group, a major bus and coach dealership based at Anston near Sheffield, was purchased for £8.5 million. In 1988 in a surprise move, Plaxton purchased the French manufacturer Carrosserie Lorraine from IVECO, but five years later had closed the company down. 1988 saw another closure, that of Seamer Road, the old plant having been made redundant following further investment at Eastfield. At the end of the decade, Plaxton acquired Henlys, a company which could trace its roots back to 1917. Ten years after it was founded, Henlys claimed to have one of the largest retail motor organisations in the country, and in west London alone, the number of showrooms and petrol stations gave the name to Henlys Corner, the junction of the North Circular Road, A1 and Finchley Road, as well as to Henlys Roundabout at the start of the A30. Over the years, Henlys expanded by a combination of acquisitions and natural growth, but the early 1980s saw a dip in car sales and in 1984 it was taken over by Hawley Goodall, the owners of hearse builders Coleman Milne. On completion of the takeover, Hawley Goodall formed a Motoring Division comprising Henlys, Mellor Coachcraft and Coleman Milne and it was this division which was purchased by the Plaxton Group. In May 1992, the Plaxton Group was renamed Henlys Group PLC and Coleman Milne was sold as part of a management buyout. The final move of the 1980s was when Arlington, one of Plaxton's original dealerships, withdrew from coach sales in 1989. Kirby acquired all of Arlington's stock, becoming Britain's biggest bus and coach dealership.

The 1990s saw Henlys purchase Wigan-based bus bodybuilders Northern Counties and also enter the North American market with a 49 per cent share in bodybuilder Prévost, which itself then purchased Canadian business Nova Bus Corp. In 1998, Henlys agreed to purchase the well-known bus and utility vehicle manufacturer Dennis for a price of £190 million. Despite agreeing the deal with Dennis, engineering group Mayflower, owners of Scottish bus builder Walter Alexander, commenced a hostile bidding war. Volvo (who owned the remaining 51 per cent of Prevost) lent its support to Henlys and their bid was raised to £247 million, but in the end the Dennis board accepted a £269 million offer from Mayflower. To offset the disappointment of losing Dennis, Henlys expanded their North American portfolio and purchased Blue Bird, the iconic American school bus manufacturer.

In a strange twist of fate, in August 2000, Henlys entered into a joint venture with Mayflower, merging the UK operations of both companies into a new organisation known as TransBus International, Henlys holding 30 per cent of the joint venture. However, the venture was to be short-lived, and on 31 March 2004 TransBus International was put into administration. Less than three weeks later, the Plaxton part of the business was sold to a management buyout and trading resumed as Plaxton Limited. Meanwhile, the Alexander and Dennis portions of

TransBus had been purchased by a consortium which included Brian Souter and Anne Gloag of Stagecoach fame. In 2007, Alexander Dennis purchased Plaxton, bringing all three companies under common ownership for the second time in a decade and since 2019, the company has been owned by the Canadian bus manufacturer NFI Group.

Those of you who have read my previous books know that I have little interest in the faceless 'boxes' of today, so I've restricted the vehicles covered to an era which includes vehicles I either remember or drove, a time I like to think of as the classic period of the British bus and coach, so for this publication it is 1960 to the end of Panorama Elite production in 1976. As with my previous publications I have been greatly assisted in my endeavours by a select band of photographers to whom I am indebted, not only for letting me use their work, but also for having the foresight to record these vehicles in their heyday for others to enjoy so many years later. Each photographer has an initialled credit after their work, and are Alan Snatt (AS), Martyn Hearson (MH) and Richard Simons (RS). I would also like to thank James Prince for fact-checking my trivia and ensuring I wasn't talking complete rubbish at times. Finally, in the text the initials NBC refer to the National Bus Company and VCS to London Victoria coach station.

Howard Berry, Cheswardine

The Plaxton Panorama and Embassy

First launched in 1958, the Plaxton Panorama was designed at the behest of Ben Goodfellow, the General Manager of Sheffield United Tours, who was looking for a modern-looking body built specifically for mid-engined heavyweight coaches from manufacturers such as AEC and Leyland. The new Panorama (as its name suggested) sported large flat-glass rectangular windows, with an entrance ahead of the front axle and shared its front-end styling with its contemporary, the Consort. Plaxtons were so confident of the success of their new product that one of the SUT examples (appropriately named Panorama Pioneer) was entered into the British and Nice coach rallies, winning top awards at both events. The Consort remained available and was usually fitted to lightweight chassis such as the Bedford SB or Thames 570E, but in 1960 these models received their own updated body style, the Embassy, and the following year Plaxton took the opportunity to update the Panorama using the same shell as the Embassy but reducing the number of window pillars. The resulting large panoramic windows became a strong influence on the development of British coach styling for years to come. Whilst the Panorama continued to be built on heavyweight underfloor engine chassis with the Embassy on lightweight front-engined chassis, this was not exclusive and led to some variations to the basic body styles. In 1961, when the maximum length of a single-deck PSV was increased to 36 feet (11 metres) in the UK, the first such coach built was a Panorama, and delivered rather appropriately to Sheffield United Tours.

For the 1962 season, Plaxton revised the Panorama further, with deeper windows all round and a reduction in the number of window pillars on 36-foot-long versions. The front end was also redesigned, which gave the Panorama a rather 'sad-smile' look unless fitted to the increasingly popular Bedford VAL chassis, which by nature of its front-mounted radiator retained the large oval grill of earlier models. It was usually known as and badged as the Plaxton Val, but when fitted with fixed windows and forced air ventilation was sometimes simply badged as a Panorama.

For the 1964 Commercial Motor Show, Plaxton worked with the Ogle design consultancy to revamp the Panorama range, with a wide chrome-trimmed band wrapped around the front and first window bay on either side. The first window bay pillar was noticeably thicker than the others and the front grille was split horizontally in two with twin headlights either side of a panel containing ventilation louvres at the top with the actual grille on the lower part. A low-cost version was made available, and this had sliding side windows as opposed to forced air ventilation and no chrome moulding to the front portion. Apart from a handful of examples, this body style was originally only fitted to the Bedford VAM and as with its sibling the VAL, these bodies were badged as Plaxton Vam (apart from bodies fitted to a few Ford R192s, which carried no badging at all). By 1966, the original Panorama had become the Panorama I and the low-cost version (which by now was available on a wider range of chassis) became the Panorama II.

Confused? Just enjoy the pictures …

The first Panoramas were delivered to Sheffield United Tours in two batches in 1958/9, all on AEC Reliance chassis, and were given names prefixed with 'Panorama'. Originally SUT 295 and named 'Panorama Paramount', 1292 WE is seen arriving at VCS in the days when the coach station was a cornucopia of colour. (AS)

One of the first operators to take coaches to the new 36-foot length was Potteries Motor Traction, and Leyland Leopard 920 UVT is seen unloading in VCS. A wonderful period picture when men wore hats and raincoats no matter the weather and a cigarette hanging from the lips was the norm. Note the nearside wiper doing a fantastic job keeping the top grille clean. (AS)

When the Panorama range was revised, bodies fitted to the popular Bedford VAL chassis retained the large oval grille, and despite being identical in outline to the Panorama was christened the Plaxton Val. Seen residing at Barton's Chilwell depot is 971 (971 SRR), a 1963 VAL14. (AS)

Another coach station, another hat and coat combination, this time worn by a very lucky man. The guard (Ribble's term for conductor) on the Blackpool-bound 745 (TRN 745), a 1961 Leyland Leopard, holds the door for the 'runner' in Preston bus station in 1973, something which I doubt very much would happen today ... (AS)

The British Shoe Corporation was formed in 1956 and until closure in 1998 was one of Leicester's major employers. To cater for the transport needs of their employees, the company operated a network of workers services using a sizable fleet of buses and coaches including 337 EWJ, an ex-Sheffield United AEC Reliance. (AS)

Another ex-SUT Reliance from the same batch was 341 EWJ, seen in the employ of Advance Roadways of Goole. It is seen parked in Christ Church, Doncaster, with a veritable feast of British and Swedish automobilia in the background. (RS)

AEC Reliance MYJ 764 seems to be having a bit of an identity crisis – Barton fleet names but Wallace Arnold livery. It was new to Dickson's of Dundee in 1962, Dickson's being bought by Wallace Arnold a year later, and MYJ passed to Barton in the early 1970s. It was one of five Panoramas delivered in 1962 (two to Dickson's, two to Epsom Coaches and one to SUT and all AEC Reliances) to be badged as Panorama Continental. Duple, who were already building a body called the Continental, raised an objection and so the Continental part was dropped. (RS)

Seen here in service with Ellisons of Ashton Keynes, Wilts, 348 XPJ was one of the two delivered to Epsom Coaches originally badged as Panorama Continentals as mentioned in the previous caption. After withdrawal, the coach remained at Ashton Keynes for several years; however, preservation didn't come a knocking and it was subsequently scrapped. (AS)

New in 1963 as a front-line coach, Northern General's AEC Reliance 2611 (PCN 11) was one of the first vehicles to receive the NBC's new two-colour dual-purpose livery to reflect its demotion to dual-purpose status. Still fit enough to travel to London, it is seen in Wembley Stadium surrounded by similarly liveried vehicles. (AS)

The Embassy and Panorama bodies had quite distinct styling differences; however, in 1963 Wallace Arnold ordered a batch of what were essentially centre entrance Panorama shells but with top sliding windows as per the Embassy and as such they received Embassy badges. Leyland Leopard 211 HUM is seen at Eastbourne's Central coach station in 1969. (AS)

Only two Plaxton-bodied vehicles were delivered new to Stratford Blue: a pair of Leyland Leopard L2s delivered in 1964. Even though it became part of the mighty Midland Red Empire in 1935, Stratford Blue was kept as a separate operating entity until 1971 when it was absorbed into the main fleet. AAC 22B is seen resplendent in its new livery when caught parked in VCS in 1972. (AS)

Vehicles operated by Blackburn-based Ribblesdale Batty-Holt all carried stainless steel Gothic script letters on their sides, as seen on 1964 AEC Reliance ACB 196B. Not all, however, had creased lower panels, which might explain why the driver doesn't look particularly happy. It is parked on Blackpool's Rigby Road coach park with the Corporation office block in the background. (RS)

I'm not sure how effective the additional fog/spotlights on Chesterfield Corporation's 16 (AWJ 689B) would be being positioned so closely together. The 1964 AEC Reliance was new to C. G. Littlewood of Sheffield, and is seen with its driver taking forty winks in Vauxhall coach park in 1972. (AS)

John Beegan of Doncaster operated a number of fascinating vehicles over the years, and whilst 2997 HL on the right, the ex-West Riding VAL, is the (supposed) focus of this picture, the amazing windscreen on TUH 120, a Weymann Beacon-bodied AEC Reliance, is surely worth a mention. Western Welsh were the only customer for the Beacon, taking all of the twenty-one built. (RS)

The early days of the NBC saw a multitude of different body styles being operated, not all of which had the corporate lettering positioned at the rear as planned. A case in point is seen on Southdown's 1180 (480 DUF), a 1964 Leyland Leopard. (AS)

Ribble seemed to have managed it though, as the NATIONAL lettering can just be seen squeezed between the waistrails on 738S (TRN 738), a Leyland Leopard allocated to the Standerwick fleet and parked on the forecourt of the old Coliseum coach station in Blackpool. I actually put this in for the background activity as much as the coach itself, with one of the ECW-bodied Bristol VRL double-deck coaches to the right and a Blackpool tram trundling down Hopton Road to the left. (AS)

Looking uncharacteristically shabby for a Black & White Motorways coach, no offside blind and having lost its characteristic B&W roof-mounted wings is AAD 245B, a 1964 Panorama-bodied Leyland Leopard. New in 1964, its condition may be explained by its being withdrawn not long after it was seen manoeuvring at home in Cheltenham. (RS)

One of the first revised Panoramas was DUD 753C, which when new in 1965 broke new ground by being Chiltern Queen's first Leyland Leopard. It was also the first vehicle in the fleet to carry a year suffix letter in its registration. It is seen with other members of the fleet in Waterloo coach park in 1968. (AS)

For many years the distinctive green-and-black-liveried coaches of Robinsons of Great Harwood were a familiar sight on the roads of Britain taking coachloads of holidaymakers from north-west England on tours across Britain. Whilst full-sized coaches were the norm, two lovely twenty-seat Embassy-bodied Bedford J2s arrived in 1965, and 130 (KTC 130C) is seen on tour in Brighton when new. (AS)

Valliant Direct Coaches of Ealing owed the unconventional spelling of its name to its Italian founders, brothers George and William Valli. The company went on to become one of the largest coach operators in the capital, undertaking contracts for the transfer of passengers between Heathrow and central London, as well as between the airport terminals themselves. Lettered for such work is Panorama-bodied AEC Reliance FLH 993C, new in 1965. (AS)

Until the company was taken over by PMT in 1987, the Staffordshire Moorland village of Brown Edge was home to Turner's, well known for their fleet of well-presented dark maroon and cream double-deckers running a regular service to Hanley via Smallthorne. New in 1965 was Embassy IV-bodied Bedford SB5 RRF 549C, the driver of which appears to have no issue with blocking the road through the village whilst he has his photo taken. (AS)

Talking of PMT, their 1965 intake included four forty-one-seat Panorama-bodied AEC Reliances to operate the company's extended tours. Six years after delivery, a rather grimy C1042 (AEH 142C) is seen parked outside Woodhouse Street depot in Stoke ready for departure to Weymouth. (AS)

Until closure in 1998, Soudley Valley Coaches was a well-respected business based in the Forest of Dean with regular services through the valley from which they took their name. They operated an eclectic fleet and were renowned for getting years of service from their meticulously maintained fleet. Nearly twenty years old when photographed in Coleford was Panorama-bodied Leyland Leopard CTH 700C, new to West Wales of Tycroes in 1965, passing to Soudley Valley in 1969. (RS)

Essex County Coaches (Galleon Tours) were loyal AEC operators, purchasing nearly eighty new Reliances until the end of production in 1979. They were also fans of the centre entrance body, with Panorama-bodied Reliance AJD 529C one of the last two coaches delivered to this configuration. (AS)

A day at Doncaster races sees Housden's of Loughborough's Panorama-bodied Bedford SB5 FDT 901C return to its old stomping ground as it was new in 1965 to Blue Ensign of Doncaster. (RS)

In 1973, Midland Red took over the business of G. Cooper and Sons of Oakengates in Shropshire. The fleet consisted entirely of Bedfords, the majority of which were stored unused until sold two years later. Seen in 1975 parked in Worcester depot is Panorama-bodied VAL14 DAW 825C, one of two identical vehicles new to Cooper in 1965. (AS)

Panorama-bodied Bedford SB13 CBK 502C was part of a batch of thirteen CBK – C registered coaches delivered to the Lancashire Motor Trader's owned fleets of Byng's of Portsmouth and Don's of Southsea. The majority were acquired when relatively new by Tappins of Didcot, who seemed to have a penchant for purchasing ex-Byng's coaches. (AS)

Back in the 1980s, National Express passengers didn't expect the high-specification luxury coaches used today, but I'm sure a few eyebrows were raised when a fifteen-year-old Bedford turned up at VCS for a duplicate back to the Midlands. Yardley (Meddings) of Birmingham's Panorama-bodied Bedford SB13 BOJ 615C was one of a pair delivered new in January 1965. (AS)

Seen at the former Booth & Fisher depot at Halfway, South Yorkshire PTE 1014 is Panorama-bodied AEC Reliance EWY 590C. New in 1965 to Felix Motors of Hatfield, it passed to SYPTE with the Felix business in 1976 and transferred to Halfway in 1978, gaining Booth & Fisher fleetnames. (RS)

Gleaming in the June sunshine we see an immaculate Panorama-bodied Reliance from the fleet of Skills of Nottingham. 55 (GTV 55D) was new in 1967 and is seen relaxing in Eastbourne's Trinity Place three years later. (AS)

When the restyled Panorama arrived in 1965, Wallace Arnold asked Plaxton to modify a batch of twelve centre entrance Embassy bodies to emulate the new model but retain the top sliding windows and roof lights of the Embassy. All were fitted to Leyland Leopard chassis and BNW 601C is seen at Wembley in 1972 carrying Bradford Northern supporters to the County Cup final. With happy passengers on board, I can only assume this is pre-match as Bradford lost to Featherstone Rovers. (AS)

On the same job as the coach above but this time on the way home judging by the faces of the passengers is Sheffield United Tours 366 (KWE 366D), a 1966 Panorama-bodied AEC Reliance. Now painted in National white livery but still with SUT's script destination blinds, it sports the later style of lower side mouldings. (AS)

Back to Tappins again, this time a new delivery, Panorama 2-bodied Bedford VAM HJB 872D. The simpler Panorama 2 was easily identifiable by the lack of front end brightwork and sliding windows in lieu of the forced air ventilation fitted to the original Panorama. (AS)

Yorkshire Traction 14 FHE 333D, a 1966 Panorama-bodied Leyland Leopard, arrives at VCS in 1968 after travelling to the capital 'via the motorway'. The coach ended its days as the 'St Barnabus', part of a fleet of vehicles operated by St Barnabas Church in Warrington, and was scrapped in 1982. (AS)

The only coach purchased new by Highland in the 1960s was Panorama-bodied Ford R226 DST 440D, originally ordered by Simpsons of Rosehearty but diverted to Highland when Northern Scottish took over Simpsons and the coach was surplus to requirements. Highland adopted the blue and grey livery for their coach fleet after buying a coach in these colours from Stanley Spencer Tours in 1966. (RS)

Manchester City Transport operated Bedford VALs on a regular service between Manchester city centre and Ringway (Manchester) Airport including 205 (GNB 518D). It later passed to Bickers of Coddenham, in whose depot it is seen in 1974. It later rose to fame as one of the four VALs used on the Beatles' Magical Mystery Tour of Liverpool and still survives awaiting restoration. (AS)

Shortly after the end of the First World War, Alfred Smith bought an ex-army lorry. His mother-in-law suggested fitting it with a charabanc body, and from these humble beginnings Smith's Luxury Coaches of Reading grew to be one of southern England's largest coach companies. Their distinctive orange and blue livery is seen to good effect on Panorama-bodied AEC Reliance MRO 140D, one of a batch new to Frames of London in 1966. (AS)

Until acquired by Greater Manchester PTE in 1976, Atherton-based Lancashire United could claim to be the UK's largest independent bus operator. They also had a tidy coach fleet which included Panorama-bodied UTC 768D, a very late L2T version of the Leyland Leopard. (AS)

No Bedford VALs were delivered new to Isle of Man operators, but sixteen were bought second hand from mainland operators. The largest fleet was that operated by Tours (Isle of Man) Ltd, who had taken over most of the Douglas-based operators including Corkill's, who were the major constituent of the Tours business. MMN 111 was originally registered FWH 354D and was new to Leigh of Bolton. (AS)

Whilst better known for operating a large network of local bus services around the Winchester area, King Alfred Motor Services also had a small coach fleet, including Plaxton Panorama-bodied VAL14 EOU 703D, seen on an excursion to Eastbourne in 1969. (AS)

W. R. and P. Bingley of Kinsley in South Yorkshire, together with fellow independents Cooper of South Elmsall and Everett of South Kirby, formed a service co-operative to run between Wakefield and Doncaster and traded as United Services. They were also prolific coach operators and in 1966 purchased two Bedford SB5s, one of which was Panorama-bodied KYG 529D. (RS)

Losing its front end brightwork and with a nasty gash to its nearside rear, Ellerby's of Tow Law's ex-Southdown Panorama-bodied Leyland Leopard EUF 222D certainly wasn't in the first flushes of youth when it was caught on camera in 1979. Having made it all the way to a rather wet London, it hadn't done too badly for a thirteen-year-old coach. (AS)

Only twenty-six Leyland Panthers were bodied as coaches for the UK market, twenty-four of them by Plaxton with the first being delivered to Soudley Valley Coaches of Cinderford in 1967. Panorama I-bodied KDF 743E is seen in 1976 on King Edward's Parade, Eastbourne. (AS)

An unusual purchase for Crosville in 1967 was a batch of ten Bedford VAMs, four of which had Panorama II bodies. Reportedly bought to compete with local excursion operators on the north Wales coast, they were subsequently downgraded to work on local express and contract work. CVT690 (NFM 690E) was the last of the Plaxtons and the only Bedford 330-engined VAM5, the other three being Leyland-engined VAM14s. (AS)

Until 1981, Glenton Tours of London specified coaches fitted with centre entrance doors had a maximum of thirty-eight seats, with each double seat staggered so that passengers had an uninterrupted view out of the window opposite. No fleet numbers were carried, as registration numbers rose consecutively with each new coach. Panorama I-bodied Reliances NYP 102E and PYM 108F are seen on London's Eccleston Bridge loading for their extended tours. (AS)

Silverline of Hounslow held numerous contracts with airlines for transfers between the terminals at Heathrow and central London. Some of these required the coaches to go airside, hence the orange beacon fitted to the roof of Panorama I-bodied AEC Reliance OLE 583E. In 1976, it was fitted with a Plaxton Supreme body for Limebourne of London. (AS)

Those who have bought my previous books know of my affection for Yelloway, so any book on Plaxtons will contain several pictures from the fleet as from 1966 until the company was sold in 1985 only two non-Plaxton bodies were purchased. Panorama I-bodied AEC Reliance HDK 507E is seen parked in Cheltenham St Margaret's coach station. (RS)

Staying with northern operators, unlike today's Manchester bus scene Droylsden-based Mayne's were for many years the only independent operator to run a stage carriage service into central Manchester in competition with Manchester Corporation. They also had a sizable coach fleet and ran numerous daily services from the Manchester area to Blackpool. For the 1967 season they took delivery of six Panorama I-bodied Bedford VAM14s including GNF 815E. (AS)

The rear-engined Daimler Roadliner was so notoriously unreliable that PMT, the largest UK customer, had two Cummins engineers permanently resident in Stoke-on-Trent assisting their engineers. Red House Motor Services of Coventry only ordered one of the locally built chassis, Panorama I-bodied KWK 220F, seen at Wembley when new in 1969. (AS)

Following their merger into National Travel South East in 1974, the garage of Samuelson's New Transport became the arrivals section of VCS and is still known affectionately as Sammy's (I wonder how many of today's National Express drivers know why). Unusually purchased second-hand from Alpha of Brighton, Embassy-bodied Bedford J2 LAY 956E is seen parked outside the depot in Eccleston Place. (AS)

Keith Coaches of Aylesbury was the coaching side of the better-known Red Rover business, both being subsidiaries of Keith Garages, which also included car dealerships. All new coaches were AEC Reliances including WBH 600E, a 1967 Panorama I-bodied AEC Reliance seen when brand new at the old Greencroft coach park just off the seafront at Eastbourne. (AS)

'Get that blind straightened …' The driver of Western Welsh 163 (JBO 163E), a 1967 Panorama I-bodied AEC Reliance, checks his manifest prior to setting off on tour to the Highlands. Fitted with a mere thirty-six seats to provide extra legroom on extended tours, the coach is seen parked in Monmouth bus station in 1971. (AS)

The dark green and black livery instantly identifies these 1967 Panorama I-bodied VAM14s as members of the Robinson's of Great Harwood fleet, whose vehicles were a familiar sight at many coastal resorts whilst undertaking the company's extended tours. The Eastbourne tour must have been particularly popular to warrant two vehicles, and sister ships 139 and 140 (ATJ 139/140E) are seen here in the town's Princes Park coach station in 1971. (AS)

Another variation on trim style, with the chrome moulding stopping at the door to allow Sutton-based Surrey Motors to apply their name. Their distinctive chocolate-and-yellow-liveried coaches were a familiar sight around the UK before the closure of the company in 1980, all licences but no vehicles passing to Epsom Coaches. (AS)

World Wide Coaches of Camberwell specialised in supplying coaches for the incoming tourist market with American Express, their biggest customer, having a 30 per cent share in the company. Seen undertaking such duties is Panorama-bodied AEC Reliance UNK 610E, one of eleven similar vehicles delivered in 1967. (AS)

A quick check left by the driver of South Wales Transport's 168 (JWN 391E), a 1967 Panorama I-bodied AEC Reliance, as he departs Cheltenham coach station for Swansea in 1975. Opened in 1932, in its heyday Cheltenham was second only to London Victoria in national importance and was famous for its 1400hrs mass departure of coaches. (AS)

Above and below: In 1967, Barton acquired the substantial business of Hall Bros of South Shields. Their modern coach fleet operated express services between the North East and the Midlands. Initially they were run as a separate entity and vehicles were given fleet numbers preceeded by the letter H, as shown on H34 (ECU 758E), a Panorama I-bodied Leyland Leopard seen at Eastbourne Central coach station on Barton's summer Saturday express service. Ex-Barton coaches were always sought after and ECU passed to another much-missed company, Cottrell's of Mitcheldean in whose depot it is seen in 1975. (AS)

The stage carriage service between Cramlington and North Shields operated by H. W. Hunter and Sons of Seaton Delaval had such a well-deserved reputation that you could virtually set your watch by a Hunter's bus. They also had several coaches, at one time either AEC or Leyland, later switching to Volvo. Sadly, the name of H. W. Hunter is now but a memory, but back in 1975 28 (LJR 749E), a 1967 Panorama I-bodied AEC Reliance, was enjoying a day at the seaside, caught on camera at Rigby Road coach park in Blackpool. (AS)

Black & White operated the UK's largest fleet of coach-bodied Daimler Roadliners, taking thirty-eight between 1967 and 1970, fitted with either Cummins or Perkins engines. One of the former was Panorama I-bodied 297 (NAD 297F), seen arriving in VCS when new in 1968. In the background is the London terminal of BOAC, passengers being transferred by a dedicated fleet of buses from there to what was at the time Croydon aerodrome. (AS)

I stand to be corrected but I believe that out of the hundreds of Bedfords operated by the Ewer Group, owners of Grey Green, this was the only Plaxton-bodied VAL. SYX 576F was new in 1968 and is seen in Eastbourne's Princes Park coach station four years later. (AS)

Eastbourne again and another Panorama-bodied VAL. Such was the popularity of Grey Green's express network that they had a pool of operators who regularly hired coaches to them. One such operator was County Coaches of Brentwood who had supplied brand-new Panorama I-bodied Bedford VAL70 TGJ 367F, seen at the old Susans Road coach station. (AS)

They do say that you never leave Eastbourne, so we're still there … Boon's of Boreham, Essex, was operating HMJ 469F, a 1968 Panorama I-bodied Bedford VAL70, when it was caught on camera at Princes Park coach park in 1973. A perfect example of a 1960s coach: plain understated livery and polished wheel trims. Lovely. (AS)

Another Essex operator to take new Panoramas was Osborne of Tollesbury. Two consecutively registered but completely different vehicles arrived in November 1967, one a Bedford VAM with a Strachan's bus body, the other 44 (XEV 187F), a Panorama II-bodied AEC Reliance. (AS)

Blackpool horse carriage operator Walter Clinton Standerwick purchased his first motor bus in 1911. Following his death, his family sold the operation to Ribble Motor Services in 1932, who amalgamated all their coaching operations under the Standerwick name. Seen turning into VCS is Panorama I-bodied Leyland Leopard FCK 937F. (AS)

Any excuse to show anther Yelloway motor, linking in nicely with the last picture as we are now in Preston bus station, Preston being where Ribble had its HQ. Flanked by Ribble Leyland Atlanteans, AEC Reliance KDK 800F departs on the X79, one of Yelloway's core Fylde coast routes. (AS)

A chassis we've not seen under a Panorama so far is the Bristol LH, available in three lengths with both the standard-length LH and long LHL both receiving Panorama bodies. Seen in the depot of Porthcawl Omnibus Co. (Kenfig Motors) is TMT 763F, new in 1968 to Golden Miller of Feltham. (AS)

New in 1968 to North Star Coaches of Stevenage, Panorama II-bodied Bedford VAM BJH 128F was an interesting choice for Barrow Corporation Transport as they weren't prolific coach operators. The reason for its 1971 acquisition was sole use by Barrow Corporation's Social Services Department, although it was owned and operated by the Transport Department. (AS)

Once a common sight at most seaside locations were coaches from local operators plying for day-trip trade on the seafront. Undertaking such a duty in Worthing for a trip to Tunbridge Wells is Southdown's 1240 (LCD 240F), a 1968 Leyland Leopard parked in front of the aptly named Southdown Restaurant. (AS)

No visit to Weston-super-Mare was complete without a visit to the coach park to see the wide variety of vehicles visiting for the day. Despite being only eight years old, Llynfi Motors of Maesteg's 128 (TRK 6F), a 1968 Leyland Leopard new to Hall's Silverline of Hounslow, looks decidedly down at heel, or maybe it's just the missing wheel trim that does it ... (AS)

Established in 1947, Edward Thomas of West Ewell were well known in AEC circles for their AEC Reliance rebodies, but between 1969 and 1971 took delivery of two brand-new Plaxton-bodied examples each year. One of the 1969 deliveries was XPL 223G, a Panorama II, a special build for Edward Thomas, built alongside the new Panorama Elite. (AS)

Talking of rebodies, the chassis on the thirty-strong batch of WHA – H registered Panorama-bodied Leyland Leopards delivered to Midland Red in 1970 must have been particularly robust as nine of them were subject to this procedure. Sadly, 6239 (WHA 239H) wasn't one of them, but is seen here when only a month old parked in Wheelwrights coach park, Gloucester Market. These were also a special build. Although looking like Panorama IIs without the fluting around the front, they were actually Panorama Is as they have forced air and fixed windows. Plaxton described them as Panorama I lightweight composite with modified moulding lines. Oddly, Midland Red had taken a batch of Panorama Elites the previous year and the reason a fair few of the WHA batch were rebodied was because the body dated very quickly but the chassis were still fine. (AS)

Charles Rickards set up business in London as a horse-cab owner expanding into the operation of various kinds of horse-drawn carriages. In 1894, he was appointed as Posting Master to Queen Victoria and in 1936 was awarded the Royal Warrant. The Royal Crest can be seen proudly displayed on MUR 209H, an Embassy-bodied Bedford J2, parked at Heathrow Airport whilst operating the Railair Link to High Wycombe, which was operated by Rickards for many years. (AS)

Another little Embassy-bodied Bedford J2 was Wallace Arnold's AUM 912J. As well as the main fleet based in Leeds, Wallace Arnold also had an operation based in the Devon resort of Torquay. As their nearest rivals were Grey Cars (who by their very name had a grey livery), Devon-based vehicles were painted in an attractive cream livery to distinguish them from the 'competition'. During the winter of 1971, AUM was converted from petrol to diesel engine as the petrol engine was considered to be too noisy. (AS)

Robert Armstrong operated in the Westerhope area, north-west of Newcastle, and developed into a leading coach operator, taking control of Galleys Coaches Ltd. The combined fleets were taken over by Tyneside PTE in 1973 and became its Armstrong-Galley coach division. New in 1970, Bedford SB5 54 (WJR 854J) shows no indication of its new ownership when caught outside Newcastle station. (AS)

Another, rather more high-profile 'takeover' was that of David MacBrayne, passing into the hands of the Scottish Transport Group in July 1969. The majority of MacBrayne's bus operations passed to Highland Scottish and included CD90 (WGE 71H), a 1970 Bedford SB5, seen in Oban. (AS)

Marchant's of Cheltenham's Ford Thames 676E EAD 75C was bought new by the company in 1965 and went on to give nearly fifteen years' service before being sent for scrap. With a 1979 Supreme IV back-end creeping into the left of the picture, EAD was probably on its last legs when caught in Cheltenham's Royal Well bus station. (RS)

York Pullman was founded in 1926 as a partnership including the wonderfully named Hartas Foxton and in just over ten years had three depots in the area. The company expanded steadily and by the 1970s was the largest tour and excursion operator in York. Seen waiting time in Navigation Road depot is MVY 586F, one of two Panorama II-bodied Bedford VAMs purchased in 1968. (RS)

The way things used to be – air conditioning provided by the open door and the driver enjoying a well-earned cigarette … With nothing to indicate its ownership, Silcox of Pembroke Dock's Leyland Leopard MDE 914F has just left the Black & White coach station in Cheltenham on National Express service 630 to Tenby. The choice of the lower-cost Panorama II coachwork (with sliding widows instead of forced air ventilation, and simplified external brightwork) was unusual on a heavyweight chassis. (RS)

The Plaxton Panorama Elite

In 1961, when the maximum length of a single-deck PSV was increased to 36 feet (11 metres) in the UK, the first such coach built was a Plaxton Panorama, delivered rather appropriately to Sheffield United Tours, the company at whose behest the Panorama was conceived. During the course of its life, the Panorama had undergone several design changes, but towards the end of the 1960s the team at Seamer Road were looking at styling the next generation of bodies, and with the maximum length of a PSV about to be increased again, this time to 39 feet (12 metres), they wanted to retain their market-leading position. The result was the Panorama Elite, stylish, with long sleek lines and a feature never before seen on a British coach – gasket glazed curved side windows. Whilst curved side windows had been a feature of cars for several years by then, their use on a coach was groundbreaking, and the Panorama Elite, with its large side windows curving gently towards the roof, set the pattern for coach design for decades to come. Launched at the 1968 Commercial Motor Show, the Panorama Elite used the large, dished taillights and front grille of the Panorama, but the interior made more use of laminate than before, with all the panels, racks and frontal area using it. The driving area was also improved, with a panel of illuminated rocker switches situated in front of the driver (previous dashboards having unlit switches in places which were inaccessible whilst moving). Two years later in 1970 the Panorama Elite II range was launched, the major external difference being the front grille, which was less curved at the corners and moulded into the side mouldings rather than finishing above it as on the original. Numerous interior changes took place to improve both passenger and driver comfort. The final incarnation of the range, the Panorama Elite III, arrived in 1972 and this time the changes were less subtle. Changes in legislation saw the emergency door moved from the front to the rear (however, some early Mark IIIs were completed with front emergency doors) and the rear lights lost their large round dish-style lights in favour of vertical 'coffin' style lights (a design that would remain through to the Plaxton Supreme IV body style). In order to meet the requirements of the government's new Bus Grant scheme, whereby operators could receive a payment of 25 per cent (later rising to 50 per cent) of a new vehicle providing it was suitable for, and spent a large proportion of its early days, working on stage carriage work, Plaxton introduced the Panorama Elite Express, complete with vertically split and powered bus specification front doors and wider entrance step with destination blind equipment fitted into an aperture in the front grille. For chassis such as the Bristol RE that were fitted with a front-mounted radiator, the destination equipment was fitted into a roof-mounted aperture which by default became known as 'the Bristol Dome'. Even though all three versions of the Panorama Elite were built to Express specification, only Elite II and IIIs actually carried the 'Express' name on the body.

Well, I might as well start this chapter with the best. With Yelloway buying new coaches every year it stood to reason they would be one of the first operators of the Panorama Elite. The 1969 intake was six AEC Reliances (what else!) including NDK 166G. They were the only Panorama Elites to carry the Yelloway logo on the lower panel as it was originally too deep to fit under the side window; subsequent deliveries had the logo reduced in size. (AS)

Both the Panorama Elite and its successor the Supreme could be ordered with additional brightwork on the lower panels, as can be seen on Byng's of Portsmouth's TGA 134G, a Leyland Leopard PSU3 new to Cotters of Glasgow in 1969. Seen at Princes Park coach park in Eastbourne, the brightwork looks remarkably undamaged considering the coach was eight years old. (AS)

A good comparison shot to see the front-end differences between the Panorama Elite I and II with two examples from the fleet of Archway Motors of Shifnal, Shropshire. Despite being three years older, Bedford VAL MVM 824G on the left looks much smarter than AEC Reliance HPP 861K on the right. The majority of Archway's fleet carried their previous operator's livery, so its pure chance that these two are in roughly the same colours. Remarkably, when Archway was taken over by Shearings in 1990, the VAL was still operational. (MH)

The immaculate fleet of Surrey Motors, Sutton, operated nearly fifty AECs during their existence and the chocolate and yellow vehicles were a familiar sight until 1980, when the decision was made by the company to cease coaching operations. WYP 203G was a 1969 AEC Reliance with a forty-one-seat Panorama Elite body. It is seen when brand new at the old Central coach station in Eastbourne. In 1973, WYP was written off following severe accident damage and passed to that lover of rebodies Edward Thomas of West Ewell, where it entered service in 1974 fitted with a new Plaxton body. (AS)

Formed in London in 1899, Birch Brothers was the first to operate a regular service from London on the newly opened M1 motorway. Sadly, a decline in passenger numbers saw the coaching operations sold to the Ewer Group in 1971. Running empty to commence the Grey Green East Anglian Express service to Great Yarmouth is Bristol LHL WLT 579G, one of three supplied new to Grey Green in 1969. (AS)

Another Bristol LHL, this time operated by a company which could have been classed as my 'local' large operator, even though they were around 15 miles away – and in another county – ahh, the joys of living in the middle of nowhere! Bassett's of Tittensor were renowned for the long lives achieved by members of their haulage and coaching fleets. They also had a penchant for buying coaches from the highly regarded Robinson's of Great Harwood, including eight of Robinson's nineteen Panorama Elite-bodied Bristols. RNR 153G, complete with Bassett's winged emblem on the front, is seen arriving at Wembley Stadium. (AS)

The World Wide fleet contained a number of rare coaches including ONK 657H, the sole completely Plaxton-built Panorama Elite-bodied Mercedes-Benz 0302. It is seen partaking in the 1970 Brighton Coach Rally with only the three-pointed star giving away the marque of its chassis. (AS)

Above and below: Due to AS not moving from his well-chosen spot outside the Southdown depot in Cavendish Place, Eastbourne, we are able to compare the 10- and 11-metre versions of the Panorama Elite. Both coaches were part of London Country's Green Line division, both were new to and transferred from the Timpsons of Catford fleet and both are AEC Reliances. Seen here operating on behalf of National Travel, P6 (BLA 593H), the 10-metre motor, was arriving to start its journey home whilst its longer sister, P8 (BLA 596H), was passing through on the way to Hastings. (AS)

Above left: BAN 115H was new to Glenton in 1970 and is seen when brand new picking up on Eccleston Bridge, London, at the start of a tour of Britain. No bright colours, no garish fleet livery, yet the little AEC Reliance just oozes refinement and class, topped off by the smartly uniformed driver. (AS)

Above right: Today we have many ways of travelling between central London and its airports but prior to this, the airlines operated several central London air terminals where passengers were checked in and then transferred to the airports by bus. By the time this photograph was taken, the BOAC fleet consisted of coach-seated Leyland Atlanteans, several of which can be seen parked in what was originally the Imperial Airways Empire Terminal, visible behind AYU 470H. The 1970 Leyland Leopard was owned by Samuelsons and was itself a matter of minutes from home. (AS)

With the introduction of the NBC corporate livery, subsidiary companies were expected to paint buses either leaf green or poppy red. There were of course one or two who decided to buck the trend including one of the smallest, Jones of Aberbeeg, a forty-vehicle-strong South Wales independent which was sold to the NBC in April 1969. For the next twelve years, and despite being under the control of Red & White, vehicles in the Jones fleet were painted blue. New to Rhondda, Leyland Leopard YTX 324H rests outside the Samuelsons garage in Eccleston Place. (AS)

Above and below: A battle of roaring engine power if ever there was one! Both had an impressive 0–60 time and top speeds of over 100 mph, but one was undoubtedly more reliable than the other. Racing up Buckingham Palace Road we have a Triumph Vitesse 2 Litre with a claimed top speed of 104 mph and 0–60 time of eleven seconds, and RDG 300G, the first of Black & White's Panorama Elite-bodied Daimler Roadliners. Their reliability (or rather lack of it) saw them lead relatively short lives at Black & White but they managed to find new homes quite quickly. RDG 300G passed to Richards of Brynmawr and is seen passing through Moreton in Marsh. (AS/RS)

That extensive list of places on the sides of Excelsior of Bournemouth's coaches always used to fascinate me, as I always wondered why anyone would want to travel to such distant locations on a Ford! But go there they did, 1968 seeing Excelsior's Managing Director Vernon Maitland taking a Panorama Elite-bodied R226 to India and back twice in fifty days. A little bit closer to home, however, is SEL 679H, a 1970 Ford R192 parked on Madeira Drive, Brighton. (AS)

Above left: National Welsh inherited Red & White's unusual fleet numbering system, which consisted of a class identifier (usually one or two letters), then the number of the bus in the batch and then two numbers identifying the year of purchase. UD7.70 (SKG 184H), a 1970 Leyland Leopard new to Western Welsh, is loading in Eastbourne ready to head home, not bad going for a coach that was ten years old when caught on camera. The stop at Severn Bridge (for connections) would more than likely be at the old Aust Services, reputed to have had the largest public cafeteria in the UK. (AS)

Above right: Shamrock & Rambler on the other hand preferred names to fleet numbers, and over the years batches of coaches carried names of composers, Roman towns, and in the case of our subject here, French towns. When the company became part of National Travel South West the namings continued but coaches also received fleet numbers in common with the rest of the division. No doubt with the driver asleep on the back seat – hence the rather rudimentary air conditioning setup – Leyland Leopard KCK 976H (Cherbourg) was one of several similar vehicles transferred from Ribble. (AS)

Above and below: As mentioned in the chapter introduction, Plaxton was the first manufacturer to offer a coach body specifically designed to meet the requirements of the UK government's Bus Grant scheme. One of the first operators to purchase the Elite Express was Barton of Chilwell, and by the end of the scheme in 1984 they had purchased nearly 350 Plaxton bodies fitted out to express specification. The original batch were all AEC Reliances and seen here are DAL 776J, on tour when brand new, and DAL 773J, still in superb condition after being sold to Beeston of Hadleigh. (AS)

One of Stonier of Goldenhill's more rural routes served the fairly large but quite isolated community of Biddulph Moor and was originally run as a works service to Chatterley Whitfield Colliery. After closure of the pit, it effectively became useless but following cuts by PMT, the local NBC subsidiary, Stonier's service was converted to carry ordinary passengers. Here we see Leyland Leopard MPR 537H at Rock End on its way to Hanley. (MH)

Fussey by name and looking at the immaculate condition of Bedford VAL70 MPR 534H, probably fussy by nature as well. New to Rendell of Parkstone in 1970, the coach is seen heading away from Doncaster Rovers' old ground at Low Pastures, which (pointless trivia time) once had a capacity of 40,000 but various safety restrictions saw this drop dramatically to just over 7,000. (RS)

In 1973, Derby Corporation acquired the fleet of Tailby & George (Blue Bus Services) of Willington. Three years later, the majority of the Blue Bus Services fleet (and depot) was destroyed by fire. Two 1966 Panorama-bodied AEC Reliances were acquired from Yelloway to help replace the decimated fleet, and so impressed was the Derby management that a third ex-Yelloway coach arrived in 1979. Despite the loss of Willington depot, the Blue Bus Services name was retained for Derby's coaching arm, as seen on PDK 463H, parked at the back of Ascot Drive depot in Derby. (RS)

I remember this coach taking us on our fortnightly school trip to the swimming baths, the only pleasurable part of the morning! Parked in a cobbled Bedminster backstreet, Leyland Leopard ONK 644H was owned by the company bearing the name of that particular Bristol suburb but was new to World Wide. Just love that it's double parked next to the Jag by the 'no parking please' sign. (RS)

Some things never change: you can still catch the Reading–Heathrow Railair link today, although you'd not be travelling on a Bristol RE. The four coaches in this batch (CJB 587–90J) worked solely on the service, so it's possible that the narrow 'Bristol dome' destination blind had no other locations on it. When their Railair days were over, all received National white livery, their destination apertures being rebuilt to full width. We are now into the era of the Panorama Elite II, identifiable by the front grille's top corners moulding neatly into the side trims rather than above them. (AS)

What an absolute beast! WJG 471J was one of East Kent's first 12-metre coaches but despite the extra length they were fifty-three-seaters to allow a bit of extra legroom on tours. It's seen entering London Victoria coach station in 1973 and despite being well into the NBC corporate livery era, still retained East Kent's traditional maroon and cream. (AS)

There weren't many Bedford VALs to receive NBC white, and I'm pretty sure that SDL 743J was one of only two Panorama Elites, the other being sister SDL 744J. Both were new to Southern Vectis in 1970 and remained until 1982, finishing their island days as part of the company's Fountain Coaches fleet. (AS)

The management team at Jones of Aberbeeg must have taken great delight in not doing things the 'NBC' way – I don't think I've ever seen a National white coach with stickers on the front, let alone as many as RC70.71 (XWO 938J) is sporting. The 1971 Bristol RELH6L is sitting well down on its haunches as the driver powers off St James Barton roundabout on the approach to Bristol Marlborough Street coach station. (AS)

At the start of the 1981 season, Southdown repainted several of their former thirty-two-seat touring coaches back into the company's traditional green livery (having been the last Southdown coaches delivered new in this livery) to undertake promotional and excursion work. 1835 (UUF 335J), a 1971 Leyland Leopard is seen at the former Cavendish Place coach station/depot in Eastbourne. (AS)

In 1982 when operators were buying brand-new, high-floor, air-suspended executive coaches, Southdown chose ten-year-old Panorama Elite-bodied leaf-sprung Leyland Leopard UUF 329J to become 'The Southdown Diplomat', converting it to fifteen-seat full-executive specification. When Brighton & Hove was separated from Southdown in readiness for privatisation, UUF 329J transferred to the Brighton & Hove fleet where it was re-registered to 408 DCD (formerly on a Southdown Northern Counties bodied Leyland PD3), upseated to thirty-two pullman-style seats and named 'The Brighton Belle'. The coach still exists and retains its executive layout. (AS)

Another coach very much with us and coincidentally also retrofitted to a luxury specification is EUU 117J. It's also a coach I've done a fair few miles in and drives beautifully due to the fact it's lived a charmed life. As can be seen, it is an AEC Reliance and was new to Glenton. It later passed to The Regency Road Pullman Touring Co. where in 2012, at the age of forty-two, it undertook a 3,000-mile tour to Russia. Subsequently restored by Go-Goodwins, it still earns its keep with O.K. Motor Services of Cambridge.

Back when the Malta bus scene was worth going over to look at, several Panorama Elites were in service as route buses. Originally FNL 581L and new to Moor-Dale of Newcastle, DBY 453 proudly proclaims its bodybuilders' heritage. The bus remained in service until the end of 'proper' route bus operation, by which time it had gained the letters PANO and RAMA across both windscreens. Despite the (extremely rare) Leyland Panther badge on the front grille, it is a Bedford YRQ, but as with many of the Malta buses it may well have received a Leyland engine as per the signwriting on the front. (RS)

Guards Tours of London was founded in 1970 by a former Grenadier Guardsman who, not wanting to do things by halves, bought his first coaches brand new, a pair of Bedford VAMs. Business must have been good as they were followed a year later by no fewer than seven Panorama Elite-bodied VAL70s including TAR 188J, seen rounding Parliament Square. (AS)

In 1975, Greater Manchester PTE took over the well-respected Bury operator Warburtons. No coaches came across, so four of GMPTE's own fleet received Warburtons Travel names, as seen on Leyland Leopard 51 (TXJ 538K) parked at Wembley Stadium in 1978. Note that it has received a slatted front grille panel of the type usually found on front-engined coaches, maybe due to the majority of GMPTE's other Panorama Elites being Seddon Pennine IVs. (AS)

In the previous caption I referred to the Seddon Pennine IV being front engined, and as such it had a large cross member which braced and supported things under the front. Panorama Elites fitted to Seddons tended to have a deeper front to help cover the crossmember, but HWT 584J from the Easton's fleet doesn't appear to be so fitted. The coach is parked on what at the time was Easton's depot at Cromer before they moved closer to Norwich. Easton's replaced the throaty Perkins V8, which gave these Seddons much of their character with a Leyland 400. (MH)

The ultimate blinged Panorama Elite? Arun Coaches of Horsham ran a rather eclectic fleet, which included one of the majestic ex-Ribble ECW-bodied Bristol VRLL double-deck coaches but ARU 80A was just as impressive. New to Greenslades of Exeter as UFJ 229J, it received a Supreme IV front end (quite a widespread practice in the late eighties as operators looked for a relatively cheap way to modernise their coaches) whilst with Eagle of Bristol. The addition of the airhorns, stainless steel wheel trims and sun visor just add to its exceptionally good condition. (MH)

The only other Panorama Elites we have seen with unusual top sliding windows were the two Southdown examples a few pages back and it wasn't until I looked closely that I realised this was one of the same batch! When only four years old, four of them were transferred to National Travel North East where they were upseated to forty-nine and put onto National Travel work. UUF 324J is seen in Derby in 1977 after National Travel North East was renamed to National Travel East. (RS)

In 1972 Barton purchased ten AEC Reliances fitted with sixty-four bus-seated Panorama Elite Express bodies, the seats configured in a 3 + 2 layout. The ten were referred to as 'jumbos' for obvious reasons, and it was probably a little bit snug with so many seats in an 11-metre body. All were sold to London Country when seven years old where they became the RN class with RN2 (MRR 802K) seen here on layover between school services. (AS)

Now one of the west of England's largest coach operators, Bakers of Weston-super-Mare made some pretty shrewd business decisions in their formative years, not least building a coach station on Weston seafront. It was ideally placed for picking up passing trade for their daily excursions, as seen being operated by WKR 101J, a 1971 Ford R226. Despite the major redevelopment of Weston seafront, the coach station is still there, although now used as parking for an adjacent takeaway. (RS)

The Supreme IV front end really did liven up an ageing Panorama Elite, especially when fitted with the chrome GT grille. With brightwork gleaming despite the snowy conditions, we see Eagre of Gainsborough's 411 HAT, a 1971 Leyland Leopard new as GYK 474J. New to Samuelsons, it did the rounds, passing to National Travel South East and then United. (RS)

The advertising budget for the Dynair Thermo Fan Drive was obviously not up to much if all they could afford was a handwritten sheet stuck in the windscreen of Salopia of Whitchurch's Ford R226 YAW 204K, the first of ten identical coaches delivered to the Shropshire firm in 1972. Telma on the other hand had splashed out on a proper poster to go in the front of the Byng's coach behind. (AS)

Despite both being heavily involved in stage carriage work across their Essex heartland, Hedingham Omnibuses and Eastern National had a harmonious relationship, borne out by TTW 675K running on hire to Eastern National. The 10-metre Bedford YRQ has a Panorama Elite Express II body, ideal for working the X24 Southend to Ramsgate service. (AS)

RTW 165K was one of the new Ford R1114 demonstration vehicles and so determined was Ford to break into the Bedford/Leyland stronghold of the Ewer Group that it was painted into Grey Green livery and sent on extended loan. It obviously didn't have much of an impact as only eight R1114s were purchased, which included five in 1978 for the recently acquired Dix of Dagenham fleet, which (by nature of its location) was almost 100 per cent Ford. (AS)

1972 saw the introduction of the Panorama Elite III, a major external difference being the rear lights, which changed from being the dished round affairs carried over from the original Panorama to what became known as the vertical 'coffin lid' style. Warrington Corporation purchased two of the earliest examples, a pair of Leyland Leopards fitted with Elite Express bodies. Both would subsequently operate for Derby City Transport, being swapped for a trio of Daimler Fleetlines. (AS)

Despite being established in 1949 when father and son Percy and Maurice Phillipson purchased an eleven-year-old Albion Victor, it wasn't until 1971 that Dearneways of Goldthorpe purchased their first new coach. They obviously got a taste for that lovely smell of a new Plaxton as from then on until the company was purchased by South Yorkshire PTE in 1981 they bought at least one new Plaxton-bodied Leyland Leopard every year. 1972 saw two arrive including NWX 874K. (AS)

Hanworth Acorn Coaches of Bedfont quite liked registration numbers all the same number or ending in two zeros. They also had a liking for the Seddon Pennine, purchasing eighteen over a five-year period, so combining the two and parked on Buckingham Palace Road is LGJ 444K, a 1972 Pennine VI. By the time this picture was taken, Hanworth Acorn had closed, and the coach had passed to Neale of Hampton, who were operating it on the London Transport Sightseeing Tour. (AS)

Now part of the National Travel South East fleet but new to Tilling's, Bristol RE PWC 344K was one of a small batch of Panorama Elites kitted out for continental tour work. As well as having only forty-four reclining seats, they were also fitted with air conditioning. Operating on behalf of Global tours of London and suitably adorned for a visit to the Dutch bulb fields, it is seen at Victoria coach station in London in 1976. (AS)

Also operating for National Travel South East on a 'continental' contract but this time staying firmly on this side of the water is Leyland Leopard GYK472J. New to Samuelsons, it is seen on Buckingham Palace Road in London and ran between central London and Dover to provide a link to the Seaspeed hovercraft service. (AS)

The origins of Delaine of Bourne in Lincolnshire can be traced back to 1890 when the family introduced horse-drawn vehicles to cater for local people wishing to travel to markets throughout the surrounding area. For years they standardised on Bedfords for their single-deck buses and coaches and VAL 70 UTL 283K, purchased in 1972, was the last VAL delivered to them, the model being discontinued the following year. (RS)

Formed in 1921, Felix of Stanley's name came from a popular song of the day, 'Felix Kept on Walking', and the black cat image was used by the company until 2009. Earlier that year, a large American company named Felix the Cat Creations Inc. advised Felix that it owned the copyright to all images of cats used next to the Felix name, and unable to afford to fight a court case, Felix removed the image from their vehicles. Bedford YRQ VNU 484K is seen in Derby bus station operating Felix's core Derby to Ilkeston route. (RS)

Leyland Leopards were very much a minority in the Great Yarmouth-based Caroline Seagull fleet, but two prepare to set out with a tour from the seafront. BPT 670L and RUP 386M were both new to County Durham independent Trimdon Motor Services – almost a matching pair apart from trim differences and repositioned emergency exit. (MH)

One of the perks of the Bus Grant scheme was that the primarily stage carriage-orientated municipal fleets could now add more luxurious vehicles to their fleets for use on private hires but still be able to easily comply with their purchase conditions. One such example was MUG 520L, one of three Leyland Leopards purchased by Leeds City Transport in 1973. By now the BOAC terminal (and some of the buses) had received British Airways branding. (AS)

The Commercial Motor Show usually held annually at Earls Court was the opportunity for manufacturers to showcase their new products and Plaxton were keen attendees. The 1972 event allowed them to present the new Panorama Elite III and as well as displaying an AEC Reliance for Best of London, they also had this lovely Bedford YRQ in demonstration livery. It subsequently became UTE 322L with Woodward of Shaw. (AS)

Formed originally to cater for the needs of the London tourist market, the attractive red-, orange-and-yellow-liveried coaches operated by Derek Randall became a more familiar sight on the Continent as the company was one of the leading lights in the 1980s European shuttle market. Unfortunately, the need to have the best coaches whilst charging competitive rates led to the demise of the company in 1985. Before the switch to DAF and Scania power the fleet was entirely AEC including 8 (MUR 214L), which survived well into the 1990s as a training vehicle with Stagecoach in South Wales. (AS)

Before PSVAR saw wheelchair-accessible coaches become the norm it was relatively rare to see a vehicle able to accommodate a wheelchair. Eastern National were one of the first operators to convert a coach to be accessible for all when 2203 (XOO 878L), a 1973 Bristol RELI I6L, was converted in 1985 to be able to accommodate seventeen seated passengers and eight wheelchairs. The central door can be clearly seen on this view taken in Chelmsford in 1986. (AS)

Another RELH originating in East Anglia was Berresford's of Cheddleton's LPW 854L, a 1973 RELH6L new to Eastern Counties. Not looking in the first flushes of youth, it is seen turning into the old Hanley bus station in 1987. (AS)

Not bad! I've managed to get this far in with only three Yelloway coaches, so let's go for a fourth. Linking in nicely with the previous picture, CDK 175L, a 1973 AEC Reliance, is seen leaving Hanley bus station with a healthy load in 1982. Yelloway vehicles racked up huge mileages on their network of North West–South West services but CDK still looks in fine fettle for a ten-year-old motor. (AS)

Another much-missed north-west England operator who also ran regular services between the Fylde coast and Manchester was Abbott's of Blackpool. Renowned for always buying new coaches with registrations ending in a 7, we see AEC Reliance NFR 497M, which had just completed a National Express duplicate journey to Leeds. (RS)

Above and below: Not many NBC coaches received the Supreme IV front update; however Eastern National did refresh a handful in 1982. As well as the new front, they also received Supreme IV side mouldings, front fog lamps, and in the case of XVW 631 and 632L to further create the illusion of being a more modern coach, the window surrounds were painted black in an attempt to emulate certain luxury coach bodies of the era. Seen not long after conversion and painted in a decidedly non-standard NBC coach livery, XVW 632L is turning into VCS. Both coaches passed to Bristol Omnibus, and when BOC was privatised they were involved in the launch day celebrations of Badgerline, the company formed to take on BOC's country area routes. Re-registered CSV 219, it is seen pulling out of Bath bus station carrying the Swift Link livery applied to vehicles usually used on limited stop services. (RS)

One of the largest independent operators in the north-west of England was the Blundell Group, owners of Smiths Happiway-Spencers. Their fleet policy was to standardise on one particular marque for several years, so AEC, Ford, and latterly Volvo featured heavily. They did, however, occasionally deviate from the norm and in 1973 purchased nineteen Seddon Pennine 6s. PEK 418L is seen parked in less than salubrious surroundings, and whilst some might say the Pennine wasn't the most refined of machines, I'm sure there's no malice intended by where it was parked ... (RS)

Western Roadways of Patchway, however, were a big fan of the Seddon Pennine and ordered fifteen over a two-year period, a combination of Pennine IV and Pennine 6 (note the return to Arabic numerals by Seddon). Here 12-metre Pennine VI 56 (HAD 289L) passes Zetland Road junction on its way into Bristol, a junction I crossed every day when changing buses to get to senior school. This was one of the last coaches purchased by Western Roadways prior to closure of the company. (RS)

The eagle-eyed amongst you will have noticed the W. E .M. S. name on the front of Bakers coach station in picture 117, the initials of Western Engineering and Motor Services Ltd, once Baker's largest competitor and taken over by Baker's in 1981. OYC 110L was one of a batch of three Ford R226s new to WEMS in 1973. (RS)

As mentioned earlier, the Ewer Group acquired Dix of Dagenham in 1976. Being based in Dagenham, the fleet was naturally biased towards Fords and despite none of the other constituents of the Ewer group operating Ford, the Dix fleet continued to receive them. New in 1973, NMJ 949M was the last Ford R226 purchased and was one of several Dix coaches on a trip to Eastbourne when captured in 1977. (AS)

Leyland Leopard TBH 33M was new to Red Rover and spent its entire life in Buckinghamshire, ending its days as SXI 6398 in the Martins Coaches fleet. Operating local bus services as well as coaches, Red Rover was ideally suited to take advantage of the Bus Grant scheme, but as with the other grant spec Elites we've seen, it's actually undertaking tour work. Nice to see a coach with a full set of badges as well. (AS)

Originally based in the tiny village of Yelverton on the edge of Dartmoor, one of Trathens' many claims to fame was importing the first Neoplan Skyliner into the UK in 1981. It's hard to believe that only seven years separate Bedford YRT OOD 381M from those impressive double-deck coaches. (AS)

It's a toss-up as to whether Smiths Happiway-Spencers was the largest operator in the North West or whether it was Shearings. Either way, they ended up under common ownership, but that era is outside the scope of this book. The Ribblesdale name was added to coaches during the 1970s as a result of a passenger pick-up agreement between Shearings and Ribblesdale of Blackburn. XMA 200M, a 1974 Ford R1114, is seen parked on Carlisle Road, Eastbourne, in 1975. (AS)

Bearing in mind the very conservative buying policy of Safeway Services (H & V Gunn) of South Petherton, it was a complete surprise when in 1974 they purchased one of the first Volvo B58s to be sold in the UK. It remained the only non-British-built vehicle to enter the fleet, subsequent purchases being Leyland Leopards and then Tigers. WYD397M is seen peering from the depot, flanked by a pair of the more usual Safeway offerings. (AS)

I mentioned earlier that ONK 657H was the only completely Plaxton-built Mercedes 0302 and here's the reason – the other one had a Mercedes front end. Another London area delivery, RWW 261M was new to Blueways (for many years suppliers of the England FC team coach) and also featured a unique 'swept-up' rear end and an attractive front-end finish to the side mouldings. It was an exhibit at the 1974 British Coach Rally and is seen here undertaking the driving skills test. (AS)

Premier of Cambridge worked closely with Yelloway on joint routes between the North West and East Anglia, and like Yelloway they also standardised on the AEC Reliance. The first Elites entered the fleet as late as 1976 and a year later the company purchased five second-hand examples, easily identifiable as they were the only coaches bought between 1972 and 1983 not kitted out to Bus Grant specification. UAR 925M was new in 1974 to Limebourne of London and entered service with Premier in 1977 after Plaxton's southern area service depot at Ware fitted it with a Bristol dome. (AS)

The coach in the background is a pure accident as I chose this picture based on Western National Bristol RE PDV 409M. When I passed my PSV test in 1988 it was down in Camborne as that was where the Western National tests were taken. I called the supervisor at Truro to give him the good news only to be told 'that's a good job boy, we were banking on you doing it because you need to bring that Bristol RE up here; we need it for traffic …' It was the very same coach and the only time I got behind the wheel of it as it was withdrawn shortly afterwards. (AS)

Staying with the National Express theme, here we have Wessex of Bristol's 367 (RHY 767M), a Leyland Leopard which was new in 1974 to Bristol Omnibus. It had a surprisingly long life at Wessex, not being withdrawn until well into the late 1980s, and is seen passing through Chippenham. It's when you see pictures like this that you remember how small the average family car was back then. (RS)

Don't know about you but I'd much rather see a coach with a proper set of manufacturer's hub covers and nut guard rings on the wheels than a set of shiny wheel trims, so this picture of Fylde's 43 (VTJ 443M) ticks my boxes. A great picture to clearly show the wide entrance and additional steps which were the main features of the Elite Express, as well as the 'pay as you enter' sign next to the door. (AS)

After buying the sixty-four-seat 'jumbos' in 1971, no more AEC Reliances entered the Barton fleet, the company instead standardising on the Bedford Y series and Leyland Leopard. One of the latter was 1428 (PAL 796M), new in 1974 and seen in Derby bus station eleven years later. (AS)

As mentioned with the Leeds Leopard a few pages back, the Bus Grant scheme was the perfect way for municipal- and council-owned fleets to operate coaches but still have a vehicle suitable for stage carriage work. One of the more colourful municipalities was Cleveland Transit, whose Leyland Leopard 379 (HEF 379N) is seen a long way from home in Blackpool's Coliseum coach station. (AS)

The story of Basil Williams' Emsworth-based Hants and Sussex Group is as entertaining as it is complicated and would take far too long to tell here. Southern Motorways was one of the many subsidiaries, and in 1975 purchased seven Elite Express-bodied Ford R1114s (including the rather spiritedly driven JNK 995N) as replacements for a batch of Bedfords fitted with some of the first Van Hool bodies to be delivered to a UK operator. (AS)

In 1975, Plaxton built the first of two batches of narrow (7 feet 6 inches wide) coaches for Greenslades of Exeter. They were built for operating tours and excursions across the West Country, primarily Dartmoor with its narrow bridges and winding roads. The first twelve were Panorama Elites and were rather disconcerting things to drive as the rear wheels protruded slightly from the bodywork, as can be seen on 325 (JFJ 505N) at rest in Exeter Paris Street coach station. The front grille and trim modifications were done shortly after entering service to overcome overheating issues. (AS)

By 1975 the continental invasion was well and truly underway with both DAF and Volvo making inroads into some very high-profile fleets. Plaxton bodied over fifty Volvo B58s that year alone including HVD 735N for Biss Brothers of Bishops Stortford. Some companies make wild claims about where their coaches go, but Biss did run a twice-weekly service from London (Marylebone Road) to Athens. Note the lack of front bumper necessitating a bracket to protect the radiator. (AS)

Sticking with the Volvo B58, here we have HYS 53N, one of the first examples delivered to the company that would go on to be the largest independent Volvo operator in the UK. To date, Park's of Hamilton (or Park's Motor Group as it is now known) have taken delivery of nearly 1,500 Volvo coaches. (AS)

Not quite what it seems. Armchair of Brentford were one of London's most respected and, by virtue of their orange and white livery, most easily identifiable companies. They were avid AEC Reliance operators; however by 1988 when this photograph was taken, they no longer operated any of their own. So, what we see here was originally HVD 739N, new to Armchair in 1975 and withdrawn in 1982. It was purchased by a gentleman named Brendan Kelly, who was a sub-hire operator to Armchair and as such it made sense to keep the coach in their colours. In order to disguise its age, he fitted a Supreme IV GT front and re-registered it to JSV 369. The tidy-looking coach is seen travelling along The Embankment in London underneath the railway out of Charing Cross station. (MH)

I mentioned earlier that I only drove one Elite-bodied Bristol RE; however the same cannot be said for the Leopard, and indeed I racked up some miles in this very motor. Western National was the only National Express contract operator based in Cornwall, so it made sense that duplication work was offered to us first. With the service work in the hands of Tigers, DAFs, Neoplans and Metroliners, we also had a fleet of Plaxton-bodied Leopards which could be turned out to do such work, usually running up to Bristol, or in this case Birmingham. 2426 (GTA 807N) seems abandoned in the middle of the old Digbeth coach station waiting for the 321 to arrive from Newcastle so it can assist as far as Plymouth. (MH)

Despite the first full-sized Supremes coming out on 'P' registration plates, numerous Elites also received the suffix letter. LBN 201P was one of a pair of Leopards delivered new to Southend Transport and were the dedicated vehicles for the X1 Southend to Heathrow service, originally a joint operation between Southend and Reading Transport and running between the two towns. (AS)

Boddy's body is back home! Not only one of the last Elites, but also one of the last AEC Reliances fitted with the 8.2-litre AH505 as this engine was discontinued shortly after KKH 833P was delivered to Boddy's of Bridlington. The coach is seen in its birthplace of Scarborough negotiating the junction between the town's railway and United bus stations, made even more difficult by the driver of the Morris Marina having made a bit of a pig's ear of stopping on the white line ... (MH)

When the Court Line Group went bankrupt in 1974 with debts of over £7 million, United Counties took on its Luton area stage carriage services, as well as eight Panorama Elite Express-bodied Ford R192s. They remained on the ex-Court Line routes, which were semi-rural and more suited to the coach seats on these vehicles. Seen here after receiving NBC livery are 201 (SXD 557L), 199 (LXD 535K) and 202 (YXD 458M). Note all three have different front grille panels. LXD was withdrawn following accident damage and was then destroyed by fire whilst in store. (AS)

What a superb picture – everything that was right from a well-respected operator in the 1970s. Three AEC Reliances from the Hutchison of Overtown fleet are seen on a visit to Blackpool. Parked in registration order are HHS 383/4/5N. Formed by Isaac Hutchison in 1922, the company grew to be one of Scotland's leading independent operators before selling to First Group in 2007. (RS)

Staying in Blackpool we see two coaches of Carruthers, New Abbey, one an Elite II, the other an Elite III. On the left, VSN 169J is a Ford R192 new to Allander, Milngavie, in 1970 and acquired by Carruthers in 1975. On the right is KOG 947P, a 1975 Leyland Leopard new to Bowen's of Birmingham as a thirty-four-seat executive coach complete with toilet. The different side trim and wiper designs between the Elite II and III can be seen. (RS)

Above and below: The seemingly evergreen front-engined Bedford SB chassis was still available, and although its market was diminishing, Plaxtons were still happy to provide a body for this chassis. The Panorama III (and subsequently Panorama IV), whilst sharing front and rear end characteristics with their Elite contemporaries, was basically unchanged from the 1960s design, retaining the flat-glass side windows of the original Panorama body. Moxon's Tours of Oldcoates SB5 Panorama III LRR 152K was new in 1972 and is seen at that year's National Coach Rally at Brighton, whilst Williamson's Billingshurst Coaches SB5 Panorama IV LWV 38P was new in 1976 and seen in their yard in 1977. (AS)

Above and below: The Panorama IV was also fitted to the Bedford VAS, the SB's smaller sibling, and was usually configured to seat twenty-nine passengers whereas when fitted to the SB chassis was normally able to accommodate forty-one. Immaculately presented and with monogrammed headrests clearly visible is VWE 454L, a VAS5 operated by the wonderfully named Reg Drabble of Sheffield. A surprise purchase by the Ewer Group in 1973 were four Panorama IV-bodied VAS5s, two for Grey Green and two for the Orange Luxury fleet. MUV 631L was the first to be delivered and so was chosen as the Ewer Group's entry in that year's Brighton Coach Rally. (RS/AS)

Rebodies and Oddities

For one reason or another, some coaches aren't destined to live long and happy lives and some (quite literally) fall apart before they reach their natural end, a bit like people really. Unlike people however, coaches can be given new bodies, so to close off here are a selection of coaches that have been given a new lease of life and a couple that were just a little different to the rest.

Now here's a chassis we've not seen before: a BMMO. In 1954, a batch of sixty-three coaches with Willowbrook bodies to BMMO design coaches were built by the Birmingham and Midland Motor Omnibus Company Ltd (the forerunners of Midland Red) and designated as BMMO C3s. Between 1962 and 1964, seventeen were lengthened and rebodied with thirty-six-seat Panorama bodywork and reclassified to type code CL3. They had Embassy-style oval grilles to ensure adequate cooling to the front-mounted radiator. I've no idea of its identity; however it can be narrowed down as only four of the batch were fitted with roof-mounted destination equipment. (AS)

Ellen Smith of Rochdale took delivery of two Leyland Royal Tiger Worldmasters: ODK 137 in 1956, which was fitted with a Plaxton Venturer body, and SDK 442 in 1958, which had a Plaxton Consort. Both were to be rebodied in later years, SDK with a Panorama Elite in 1970, and as seen here, ODK with a Panorama 1 in 1968. Can you still get Slimcea bread? (RS)

No, this isn't an early example of a cherished registration plate, MBY 347 was its real number. This AEC Reliance was new in 1954 to Bourne & Balmer and was fitted with a rare Park Royal Royalist body. It later passed to Halifax Corporation, who had it rebodied with a Panorama I in 1968. (AS)

You have to remember that the Panorama had been superseded by the Panorama Elite several years before Starr of North Anston's 1971 Reliance JWT 743J was delivered. Jack Starr disliked the Elite, so had JWT 743J built as a special order. The coach took twelve months to build as the chassis had been delivered to the factory with a set-back front axle to accommodate grant doors, and the planned body had already been assembled. After completion, it attended the Blackpool Coach Rally where, to great embarrassment, it gained more order enquiries than the Elite. (RS)

Seen visiting Doncaster Racecourse is Tatlock's of Radcliffe's AEC Reliance GBU 30K, new as 8321 U to Wallace Arnold in 1958 and fitted with Plaxton Consort coachwork. When it was rebodied in 1971, Tatlock's ensured it received a white steering wheel as sported by several of the fleet, as well as the name 'Edith IV', the Edith name also being a Tatlock's tradition. (RS)

Now here's a coach with a story to tell. WLO 692 was a Burlingham-bodied Leyland Tiger Cub new to Banfield's of London in 1955. In 1970, Banfield's sold the coach for export to Afghanistan, but it broke down en route and was returned to England. A Kent operator bought the coach with the intention of having it rebodied but ceased operating before this took place. In 1971, the chassis was acquired by Edward Thomas of West Ewell, who refurbished it and had a new Panorama Elite body fitted. It is seen on Epsom Downs on the 1974 Derby Day. Cop a look at the 'go faster' Allegro in the background ... (AS)

Probably the oldest Panorama Elite rebody was FYS 689. New to Glasgow Corporation in 1947, it was a Leyland Worldmaster RT3 with Weymann bus bodywork completed in Glasgow's own workshops. It later passed to Woods of Mirfield for use on its local bus service between Dewsbury and Mirfield. In 1972 the chassis was fitted with new Panorama Elite II coachwork as seen here. (RS)

FJP 502 was new to Smiths of Wigan in 1960 as part of a batch of six Plaxton-bodied AEC Reliances. Between 1969 and 1973, four of the six were rebodied with Panorama Elites as part of an exercise to give their engineering apprentices the opportunity to train on chassis preparation. All retained their original registration numbers apart from sister ship FJP 506, which was re-registered to GEK 809G. (AS)

My first foray into preservation was back in 1991 when I, along with three colleagues at Sanders of Holt, purchased 521 FN, sister ship to the coach seen here. New in 1962 to East Kent and fitted with Park Royal bodies, they were rebodied when ten years old. Several passed to Caroline Seagull of Great Yarmouth, who were selling Panorama Elite-bodied five Reliances when I visited. I chose 521 FN purely because it was the only one with the original AEC dashboard binnacle and to my delight (and the dismay of Caroline Seagull's owner, the wonderful Mr Buckle, who has kept in touch ever since) found that its last driver hadn't realised it was to be withdrawn and so it came complete with a full tank of fuel! (AS)

I was going to discard this as we've already had several Wallace Arnold pictures (in my defence, they did operate a lot of Plaxtons) but then I clocked its registration plate. New as a Panorama in 1968, AEC Reliance NUB 712F was involved in an accident. The coach was (like many WA coaches at the time) on long-term hire from Cleckheaton-based dealer Stanley Hughes, who decided to send the coach for rebodying and upon its return it was then purchased by WA. (AS)

Jack Starr's coaches frequently worked express services on hire to Sheffield United Tours at summer weekends, and AEC Reliance MEF 116J is seen unloading in Sheffield on return from Scarborough. New to Beeline of Hartlepool, whose livery it still carries, this is another rebody. Originally AEF 654C, its Plaxton Panorama body was removed following a rollover accident in 1970. The resulting rebuild was enough for it to be re-registered as well as rebodied. (RS)

Well, we've had a J-registered Panorama, so how about an E-registered Panorama Elite? E902 DRG was a Bedford YRT delivered to Cleckheaton dealer Jack Hughes in 1973. It was one of half a dozen vehicles which remained unsold and were discovered when Mr Hughes passed away in 1987. It was bought, together with two similarly bodied coaches (one Bedford, one Ford), by Bob Smith Travel of Langley Park, and all three were registered for the first time, hence the 'E' prefix registration. It is seen in 1994 making its way into Sheffield when owned by Serene Travel of Bedlington. It is interesting to note that it entered service a year after Bedford pulled out of the PSV market. (RS)